TIMELINE HISTORY

TRANSPORT

From Walking to High-speed Rail

Elizabeth Raum

www.raintreepublishers.co.uk
Visit our website to find out more information about Raintree books.

To order:
☎ Phone 0845 6044371
🖷 Fax +44 (0) 1865 312263
🖳 Email myorders@raintreepublishers.co.uk

Customers from outside the UK please telephone +44 1865 312262

Raintree is an imprint of Capstone Global Library Limited, a company incorporated in England and Wales having its registered office at 7 Pilgrim Street, London, EC4V 6LB – Registered company number: 6695582

Text © Capstone Global Library Limited 2011
First published in hardback in 2011
The moral rights of the proprietor have been asserted.

Edited by Louise Galpine and Diyan Leake
Designed by Richard Parker
Original illustrations © Capstone Global Library Ltd 2011
Illustrated by Jeff Edwards
Picture research by Hannah Taylor
Originated by Dot Gradations Ltd
Printed and bound in China by CTPS

ISBN 978 0 431 02553 7 (hardback)
14 13 12 11 10
10 9 8 7 6 5 4 3 2 1

British Library Cataloguing in Publication Data
Raum, Elizabeth – Transport : from walking to high-speed rail. – (Timeline history)
388'.09-dc22
A full catalogue record for this book is available from the British Library.

Acknowledgements
We would like to thank the following for permission to reproduce photographs: Alamy Images pp. **5** top (© SCPhotos), **12** (© Interfoto), **24** (© RIA Novosti); Corbis pp. **4** (Harrison Schmitt), **6** (Bettmann), **8** (Bettmann), **11** top (Fine Art Photographic Library), **14** bottom (Bettmann), **15** (Bettmann), **19** top (Bettmann), **20** (Bettmann), **22** bottom (Bettmann); Getty Images pp. **7** bottom (The Bridgeman Art Library), **10** (The Bridgeman Art Library/Look & Learn), **11** bottom (SSPL), **18** (SSPL), **19** bottom (Hulton Archive), **21** bottom (New York Times Co.), **22** top (Hulton Archive), **23** (Fox Photos/M. McNeill), **25** bottom (AFP/Simon Maina), **26** (Bloomberg/Peter Frommenwiler); Library of Congress pp. **14** top, **16** top; Mary Evans pp. **13** top (©Rue des Archives), **9** bottom, **16** bottom; NASA pp. **25** top, **27** bottom (Steve Lee University of Colorado, Jim Bell Cornell University); Photolibrary pp. **7** top (North Wind Pictures), **9** top (Steve Vidler), **13** bottom (The Print Collector), **17** (The Print Collector), **21** top, **27** top (Othk Othk).

Cover photograph of a high-speed train reproduced with permission of Shutterstock (© Aleksi Markku).

Every effort has been made to contact copyright holders of material reproduced in this book. Any omissions will be rectified in subsequent printings if notice is given to the publisher.

Contents

Historical time is divided into two major periods. BC is short for "before Christ" – that is, the time before the Christian religion began. This is the time up to the year 1 BC. AD is short for "Anno Domini". This is Latin for "in the year of our Lord", meaning the time from the year 1 BC to the present. For example, when a date is given as AD 1000, it is 1000 years after the year 1 BC. The abbreviation *c.* stands for *circa*, which is Latin for "around".

Any words appearing in the text in bold, **like this**, are explained in the glossary.

What is transport?

Transport is the way people and goods move from place to place. We travel on foot, by bicycle, or in a car. In cities, public transport includes buses, trams, and trains. Ships, planes, and spacecraft make it possible for people and goods to travel great distances.

The **Moon rover** carried astronauts across the surface of the Moon in the 1970s.

Trade

Transport allows us to trade with other people, and trade allows for the growth of towns and cities. Transport brings farm goods and building materials to the cities where they are traded for other goods. In early times, travel and trade were slow and difficult. Today, it's possible to travel all over the world by land, sea, or air.

For thousands of years, people have used boats to travel from place to place, as shown in this painting from ancient Egypt.

Timelines

The information in this book is on a timeline. A timeline shows you events from history in the order they happened. The big timeline in the middle of each page gives you details of a certain time in history (see below).

date marker

timeline

100,000 BC   50,000 BC   10,000 BC   8,000 BC

timeline break   dates

Some dates are exact. For example, in the year 1969 men first walked on the Moon. Others are more general because early people did not keep written records. The smaller timeline at the bottom of each page shows you how the page you are reading fits into history as a whole. You will read about transport all around the world. Each entry on the main timeline is in a different colour. This colour shows you which continent the information is about. The map below shows you how this colour coding works. Pale green indicates events that took place on more than one continent or worldwide.

North America

Europe

Asia

Worldwide

Africa

South America

Australia and Oceania

Beginning to travel

Early people walked great distances gathering food and hunting. Gradually, people moved from Africa to Asia and Europe. The invention of boats and wheels allowed people to travel even further and to carry heavier loads.

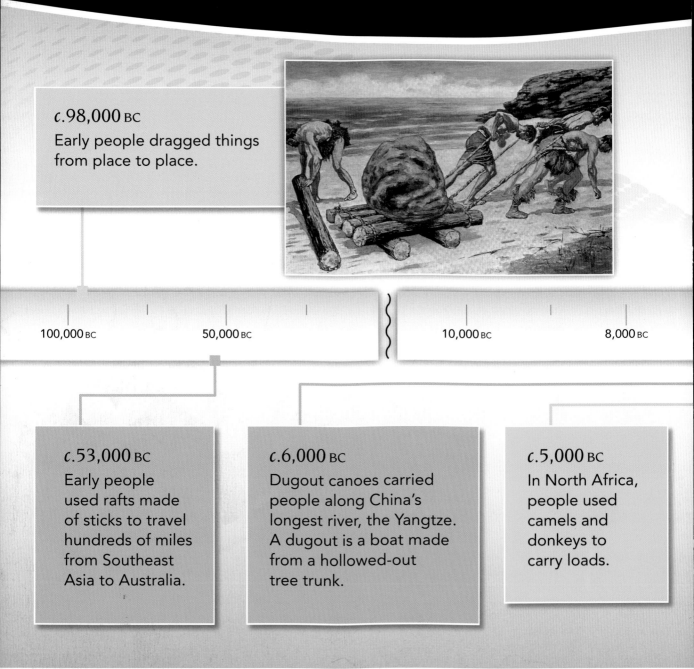

c.98,000 BC
Early people dragged things from place to place.

100,000 BC | 50,000 BC | 10,000 BC | 8,000 BC

c.53,000 BC
Early people used rafts made of sticks to travel hundreds of miles from Southeast Asia to Australia.

c.6,000 BC
Dugout canoes carried people along China's longest river, the Yangtze. A dugout is a boat made from a hollowed-out tree trunk.

c.5,000 BC
In North Africa, people used camels and donkeys to carry loads.

_c_.4,000 BC
The Phoenicians, a **civilization** in the **Middle East**, sailed the Mediterranean Sea in long wooden rowing boats with room for 15–20 rowers on each side.

_c_.3,300 BC
Egyptians tied bundles of **reeds** together to make boats. A reed roof kept sailors dry.

6,000 BC   4,000 BC   2,000 BC

_c_.3,500 BC   ROLLING ALONG
No one knows exactly when the wheel was invented. It probably began as a rolling log. People made the first wheels by tying three flat boards side by side and carving them into a circle. Later, they used stone or clay. By the 1300s BC, they were used on **chariots** in Egypt (right).

Picking up speed

By about 2000 BC, people in Egypt, China, and Scandinavia made lighter, larger wheels with **spokes**. Wheels with spokes were easier to pull long distances.

*c.*2000–1500 BC

Chariots were light, fast, two-wheeled carts pulled by horses. They helped the Egyptians win wars.

*c.*400 BC

The trireme, a high-speed wooden warship used by the Greeks and Romans, had space for 170 men to sit and row.

*c.*AD 100

The Chinese invented the **wheelbarrow**, a single-wheeled **vehicle** with handles used to carry heavy loads.

2000 BC 400 BC 200 BC 1 BC AD 200

*c.*AD 700 SPEEDY SHIPS

The Vikings lived in what is now called Denmark, Norway, and Sweden. They built speedy ships made from the wood of oak trees. Both ends of the boat often were the same so the ship did not have to turn around in narrow rivers or small harbours. Vikings used their warships to raid cities and towns throughout Europe.

c.AD 800

During the T'ang **dynasty**, Chinese traders increased the use of boats called junks to carry goods to markets abroad. Junks had a hull (lower part) that was divided into sections for **cargo**.

AD 400 AD 600 AD 800 AD 1000

c.AD 900–1000

Horses could travel farther and pull heavier loads once iron horseshoes and harnesses were improved.

Facing dangers at sea

Travelling across the world's oceans was especially dangerous for slaves and prisoners forced on to ships. At least two million Africans died on slave ships because of illness or lack of food and water.

1492
Christopher Columbus sailed from Spain to America in the *Santa Maria*, a **carrack**. His other ships, the *Niña* and the *Pinta*, were **caravels**. These ships were sturdy enough for long ocean voyages.

| 1480 | 1530 | 1580 | 1630 | 1680 |

1500s–1800s
Slave ships made over 39,000 trips from Africa to America. The trip took 2–4 months. Many millions of Africans were taken to a life of captivity.

Late 1600s–1850s OVERLAND CANALS
Until the mid-1800s, people in Europe and North America hauled supplies on barges, large flat-bottomed boats. Horses trudged along the banks of **canals** pulling the barges, which went through locks (right) when water levels changed. Workers dug the canals by hand. Early canals in England carried coal from mines to factories. By 1850, there were 7,200 kilometres (4,500 miles) of canals in the United States.

1670

In Great Britain, **stagecoaches** carried people between London and Edinburgh. The journey took two weeks. Stage coaches continued to be used in Britain into the 1900s.

1787–1868

Due to overcrowding in prisons, the British shipped 162,000 prisoners to Australia. The prisoners slept in chains and had barely enough room to stand up.

1730   1780   1830   1880

Building up steam

James Watt of Scotland invented a working steam **engine** in 1765. For **energy**, steam engines used pressure (force) created by boiling water. Other inventors used Watt's steam engine to provide power for ships, trains, and cars.

1700
Russians used horse-drawn sledges for winter travel.

1740
In New York City, in the United States, people rode in carts pulled by oxen.

1700   1720   1740   1760

1700s
Miners travelled by canoe from São Paulo to gold mines in Minas Gerais, a state that has some of the biggest rivers in Brazil. Groups of 50 to 300 canoes made the trip in 5 to 7 months.

1769
Nicolas-Joseph Cugnot of France invented a steam-powered **vehicle**. It travelled 3.6 kilometres (2¼ miles) per hour and stopped every 10–12 minutes to build up enough steam to keep going.

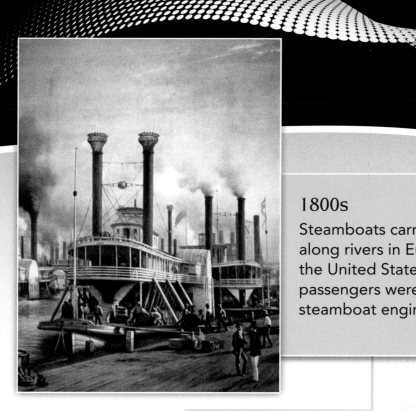

1800s

Steamboats carried passengers along rivers in Europe and the United States. Sometimes passengers were killed when steamboat engines blew up.

1780   1800   1820

1783   UP, UP, UP AND AWAY

A hot-air balloon landed in a small French village. The villagers thought it was a monster and attacked it with stones and pitchforks. Soon hot-air balloons became a regular sight. People used balloons for sightseeing, to predict the weather, and to observe enemies during wartime.

Cruising the oceans

During the mid-1800s, shipping companies offered passenger service across the oceans. Cruise ships provided nice rooms and tasty food for rich passengers. **Immigrant** ships, on the other hand, carried poor people from Europe to America. The ships were crowded and often there was not enough food and water.

1820s–1880s
Over 9.5 million immigrants reached a new life in the United States by ship.

1820 1825 1830 1835

1825
The British engineer George Stephenson built a **locomotive** called the *Rocket*. It made future railways possible.

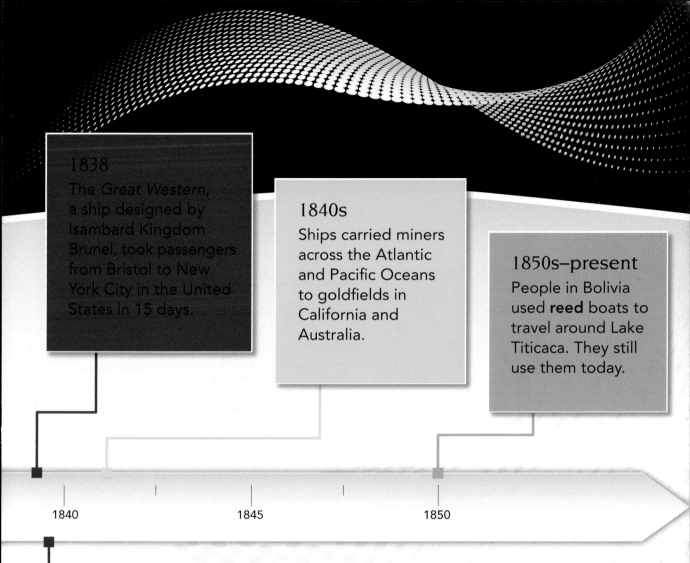

1838
The *Great Western*, a ship designed by Isambard Kingdom Brunel, took passengers from Bristol to New York City in the United States in 15 days.

1840s
Ships carried miners across the Atlantic and Pacific Oceans to goldfields in California and Australia.

1850s–present
People in Bolivia used **reed** boats to travel around Lake Titicaca. They still use them today.

1840   1845   1850

1839   BICYCLES FOR EVERYONE
A Scottish **blacksmith** called Kirkpatrick Macmillan invented the first bicycle with pedals. In 1868, rubber tyres and brakes were added. At first, adults had trouble learning to ride bicycles. Today, bicycles are used throughout the world. They are cheaper than cars and do not cause pollution.

Chugging along

During the 1800s, passenger service grew. Trains, subways, and rickshaws (two-wheeled carts that a person pulls) gave large numbers of people new ways to travel across a country or within cities.

1840–1880

In the United States, pioneers travelled by covered wagon to settle in the west of the country.

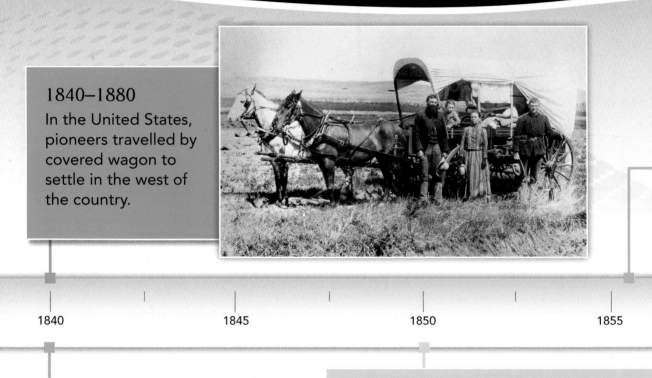

| 1840 | 1845 | 1850 | 1855 |

1840–1907

Thousands of camels were brought to Australia from Asia to transport people and goods.

1850s   OPENING UP THE WORLD

Thanks to George Stephenson's *Rocket*, passenger rail service expanded. A total of 800 kilometres (500 miles) of railway existed in the United Kingdom in 1838. By 1860, this had increased to 16,000 kilometres (10,000 miles). Train services grew throughout Europe and Asia, too. By the 1890s, trains ran from Paris in France to Istanbul in Turkey.

1850s

In India camels pulled **stagecoaches** from town to town.

1869

The rickshaw was invented in Japan. Rickshaws were an early taxi service and are still popular in countries such as India.

1860　　　　1865　　　　1870

1860–1861

Pony Express riders delivered the mail on horseback throughout the western United States. Riders could cover 400 kilometres (250 miles) a day.

1863

The London **underground** system carried 9,500,000 passengers during its first year. As cities grew, so did public transport. Today, cities such as New York, Rome, and Lisbon depend on buses, trams, and trains.

Inventing the car

The first cars were slow and costly. In the 1880s, Karl Benz and Gottlieb Daimler invented petrol **engines**. Other inventors raced to improve earlier designs. The age of the car had begun.

1885
In Germany, Gottlieb Daimler put his petrol engine on a bicycle and made a motorcycle (left). He also built a car with four wheels using the same engine.

1870   1875   1880   1885

1870s
Three times a year, 15,000 camels travelled from Azerbaijan, on the Caspian Sea, to Turkey. Camel **caravans** carried as much as seven or eight ships could carry.

1885
Karl Benz of Germany invented a three-wheeled car with a petrol engine.

1890

Bicycles became popular in Japan. Today, bicycles are used throughout the world.

1898

In the United States, the Stanley brothers' steam-powered car travelled at 56 kilometres (35 miles) per hour.

1890　　　　　　1895　　　　　　1900

1899　THE MODEL T

The US inventor Henry Ford started to make and sell cars. By 1913 they were being made on an **assembly line**, moving on a belt to workers who put the pieces together. Between 1908 and 1927, the Ford Motor Company produced half of all the cars made worldwide. By 1927, the company had made 15 million Model T cars.

Flying

Once the Wright brothers invented a workable aeroplane, pilots eagerly took to the air.

1903   WRIGHT BROTHERS

Wilbur and Orville Wright made the first successful aeroplane flight in Kitty Hawk, North Carolina in the United States. The first flight lasted 12 seconds and went only 36 metres (120 feet). This short flight led to the development of the modern aeroplane.

1903   1905   1907   1909   1911   1913   1915

1910

Henri Fabre of France built the first seaplane by removing the aeroplane's wheels and attaching floats.

1911

Cal Rodgers, a US motorcycle racer, flew an aeroplane from New York to California in 49 days. He made 30 stops and crashed 19 times.

1918–1937

Balloon-like airships – also called zeppelins, blimps, and dirigibles – carried passengers across the Atlantic Ocean. In 1937, a German airship called the *Hindenburg* burst into flames over New Jersey, USA. Thirty-six people were killed. This event brought airship passenger service to an end.

1920s

The first planes in West Africa were French mail carriers.

1917 | 1919 | 1921 | 1923 | 1925 | 1927

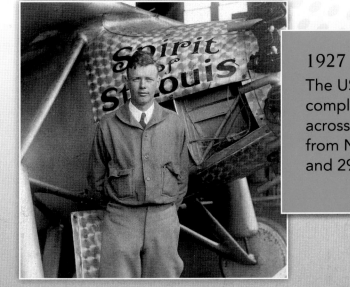

1927

The US pilot Charles Lindbergh completed the first **solo** flight across the Atlantic Ocean. He flew from New York to Paris in 33 hours and 29 minutes.

Transporting soldiers

During World War II (1939–1945), planes, ships, submarines, and trains became fighting machines. Inventors improved tanks, designed jets, and built aircraft carriers. Ships and trains transported soldiers to and from battlefields.

1930

Robert Goddard built a rocket test site in New Mexico in the United States. Rockets would later be used for spaceflight.

1930   1932   1934   1936   1938   1940   1942

1937   HELICOPTER

Igor Sikorsky, born in Russia in 1889, designed planes for the Russian Army. He moved to the United States in 1919 and designed a helicopter. By 1939 he had a working model that flew up and down as well as backwards and forwards.

1939

A German test pilot flew the first jet-powered aircraft. The most successful German jet fighter could fly over 885 kilometres (550 miles) per hour.

Late 1940s

Train tracks were repaired after World War II. Passenger services which had stopped during the war began again.

Late 1950s

Passenger air travel increased.

| 1944 | 1946 | 1948 | 1950 | 1952 | 1954 | 1956 |

1939–1945

During World War II, the United States used 30 aircraft carriers. Planes landed and took off from the decks of the ships.

1956

In the United States, construction began on a system of highways across the country. These **interstate** highways now cover 75,440 kilometres (46,876 miles).

Soaring into space

In the 1950s, the United States and the **USSR** raced to see who could send a man into space first. Today countries in North America, Europe, and Asia work together to explore space.

1961
Yuri Gagarin of the USSR became the first man to orbit the Earth.

1960   1965   1970   1975

1969
The US astronaut Neil Armstrong became the first human being to walk on the Moon.

1971
US astronauts rode a **Moon rover** across the Moon's surface.

1976
France and Britain developed the Concorde jet, which flew faster than the speed of sound. It travelled from Paris to New York in 3½ hours, twice as fast as other aeroplanes.

1981

The United States launched the first space shuttle. It could land on a runway like an aeroplane and fly again. Shuttles carry people and supplies to the International Space Station. By 2015, shuttles will be replaced by newer spaceships.

1986

The space shuttle *Challenger* exploded on take-off, killing everyone on board.

1980   1985   1990

1970s–present

People throughout Africa often rely on buses for transport. Buses can be overcrowded.

Going green

Walking, cycling, or sailing rather than flying keeps the air clean. In the future, **vehicles** may get **energy** from the Sun, wind, and magnets, rather than burning coal, petrol, or oil.

2007
Bike-makers produced twice as many bicycles as cars. China leads the world in bicycle use.

Present
Hybrid cars use electricity so they don't emit too many pollutants and petrol so they can go at the speed and distance needed.

2000   2002   2004   2006   2008

2010
The giant wings of Switzerland's Solar Impulse use the Sun's energy to power the plane.

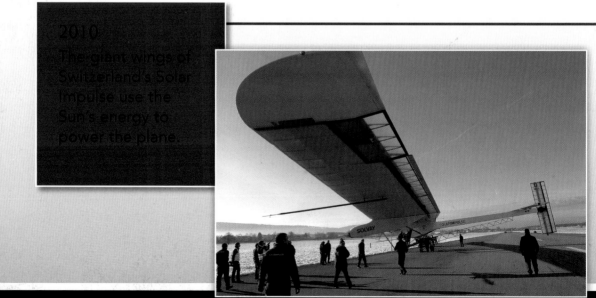

Present

Maglev (magnetic levitation) trains that operate in Japan and China are the world's fastest trains. They are called "green" trains because they use magnets for energy. Powerful magnets beneath the rail lift the train and pull it forward. By 2025, Japan plans to have a maglev train running between Tokyo and central Japan at over 500 kilometres (310 miles) per hour.

2010

Future

Present

Companies are planning the spaceships, space hotels, and space stations that tourists will need for space travel.

Future

A moving science lab named *Curiosity* will explore Mars (above). Scientists from all over the world work to invent new ways to travel in outer space.

Key dates

c.98,000 BC
Early people walk and drag items by hand.

c.6,000 BC
Dugout canoes carry people along China's longest river, the Yangtze.

c.5,000 BC
In North Africa, people use camels and donkeys to carry loads.

c.3,500 BC
Sumerians invent the wheel.

C.AD 700
Vikings make fast wooden boats.

C.AD 800
Chinese traders start to use boats called junks to carry **cargo** to market.

C.AD 900–1000
Horses travell farther and carry heavier loads once iron horseshoes and harnesses are invented.

1492
Christopher Columbus sails to America in a **carrack**.

1500s–1800s
Slave ships make over 39,000 trips from Africa to America.

Late 1600s–1800
Horses pull large flat-bottomed boats called barges along the banks of **canals**.

1700s

Miners travel by canoe to the gold mines in Minas Gerais, the state that is the source of some of the biggest rivers in Brazil.

1825

George Stephenson builds a **locomotive** called the *Rocket*.

1839

Scottish **blacksmith** Kirkpatrick Macmillan invents the bicycle.

1885

German Karl Benz invents a three-wheeled car with a petrol **engine**.

1899

Henry Ford founds his car company and sets up the **assembly line**.

1903

The Wright brothers make the first successful aeroplane flight.

1961

Russian cosmonaut Yuri Gagarin takes the first spaceflight.

1969

US astronaut Neil Armstrong walks on the Moon.

1981

The first space shuttle is launched from Florida, USA.

Present

Maglev (magnetic levitation) trains that operate in Japan and China are the world's fastest trains.

Glossary

assembly line moving belt in a factory that takes products being built to the workers for them to add the next part

blacksmith person who makes and repairs iron objects

canal long water channel built for travelling across large areas of land

caravan group of travellers journeying together for safety

caravel small Spanish or Portuguese ship with two or three masts

cargo trade goods carried on ships or other vehicles

carrack sturdy merchant ship used in the 1500s

chariot light, two-wheeled vehicle for one person, usually drawn by horses

civilization particular society or culture at a particular period of time

dynasty period of rule of a particular family

energy ability to do work

engine machine that burns fuel to turn energy into movement

immigrant person who comes to live permanently in a foreign country

interstate between different states in the United States. Interstate highways go from one state to another.

locomotive train engine that pulls carriages and other cars along

Middle East region that includes south-west Asia and north-east Africa

Moon rover four-wheeled vehicle used by astronauts on the Moon

reed straight stalk of grass

solo alone

spoke thin piece of a wheel that connects the centre to the rim

stagecoach wagon pulled by an animal, taking passengers on a set route

underground railway network that runs beneath the surface of the Earth

USSR Union of Soviet Socialist Republics. The USSR later broke up into the Russian Federation and other countries.

vehicle means of transport often having wheels or runners

wheelbarrow single-wheeled vehicle with handles, for moving heavy loads

Find out more

Books

Extreme Machines series (Raintree, 2010)

Transport: Find Out About Engines, Gravity and Flight with 40 Great Experiments and Projects **(Hands on Science series)**, Chris Oxlade (Southwater, 2008)

Transport: From the First Wheels to Special Cars **(Brain Power series)**, Penny Clarke (Book House, 2006)

Would You Believe ... Two Cyclists Invented the Aeroplane?!: and Other Transport Triumphs, Richard Platt (Oxford University Press, 2010)

Websites

Go to the "Transportation" section of this "How Everyday Things Are Made" website to learn about the design and technology behind making planes, cars, and motorbikes.

manufacturing.stanford.edu/hetm.html

These web pages provide a history of trains and how they work.

science.howstuffworks.com/train.htm

Places to visit

London Transport Museum
Covent Garden Piazza
London WC2E 7BB
Tel. 020 7565 7299
www.ltmuseum.co.uk

Coventry Transport Museum
Millennium Place
Hales Street
Coventry CV1 1JD
Tel. 024 7623 4270
enquiries@transport-museum.com

Museum of Transport
1 Bunhouse Road
Glasgow G3 8DP
Tel. 0141 287 2720

Ulster Folk & Transport Museum
Cultra
Holywood
BT18 0EU
Tel. 028 9042 8428
www.nmni.com/uftm

Index